DEC - - 1992

DUE DATE

04. AUG 93
15. FEB 94
12. MAR 94

15. FEB 96

18. JUN 96
04. FEB 97

THE OLYMPICS

Neil Duncanson

The Olympics

The publishers would like to thank the Comité Organitzador Olímpic Barcelona '92 S.A. for granting permission to use the Official Sports Pictograms of the Barcelona '92 Olympic Games (© 1989 COOB '92 S.A.) in this book.

Picture acknowledgements

The artwork on the cover and on pages 21 (above), 24, 29, 37 and 38 is by Nick Hawken.

The publishers would like to thank the following for supplying their photographs for use as illustrations in this book: Allsport *cover* 5 right (Pascal Rondeau), 7 (Joe Patronite, 9 (Mike Powell), 10 (Billy Stickland), 11 (Mike Powell), 12 (Steve Powell), 13, 14 left (Mike Powell), 15 (Billy Stickland), 17 (Bob Martin), 17 left, 17 right (Kit Houghton), 18 (Tony Duffy), 19 left (Mike Powell), 19 right (Joe Patronite), 20, 21 below (Bob Martin), 22 (Tony Duffy), 23 (Steve Powell), 25 left (Gray Mortimore), 25 right (Tony Duffy), 26, 27 above, 27 below (Mike Powell), 28 (Tony Duffy), 29 (Tony Duffy), 30, 31 (Mike Powell), 32 (Billy Stickland), 33 left (Gray Mortimore), 33 right (Tony Duffy), 34 (Russell Cheyne), 35 left (Simon Bruty), 37 right (Steve Powell), 39 below (Simon Bruty), 40 (Joe Patronite), 41 left (Tony Duffy), 41 right, 42 (Tony Duffy), 43 left and right, 44 (Bill Frakes), 45 (Gray Mortimore); Mansell 5 left; Popperfoto 6, 8, 14 right, 36; Ronald Sheridan 4; Topham/Associated Press 35 right, 39 above.

Designer: Joyce Chester
Editors: William Wharfe/Paul Bennett

First published in 1991
by Wayland (Publishers) Ltd
61 Western Road, Hove
East Sussex, BN3 1JD, England

© Copyright 1991 Wayland (Publishers) Ltd

British Library Cataloguing in Publication Data
Duncanson, Neil
  The Olympics.
  I. Title
  796.48

HARDBACK ISBN 1 85210 325 6

PAPERBACK ISBN 0 7502 0242 4

Typeset by Dorchester Typesetting Group Ltd
Printed in Italy by Rotolito Lombarda S.p.A., Milan
Bound in Belgium by Casterman S.A.

Contents

The Olympic dream	4	Marathon	30
Basketball	6	Middle-distance running	32
Boxing	8	Modern pentathlon	34
Cycling	10	Pole vault	36
Decathlon/Heptathlon	12	Rowing	38
Distance running	14	Sprinting	40
Equestrian events	16	Swimming	42
Gymnastics	18	Carrying the flame	44
High jump	20	The Olympic events	46
Hurdles	22		
Javelin	24	Glossary	47
Judo	26	Further reading	47
Long jump	28	Index	48

The Olympic dream

When more than 160 nations march into Barcelona's breathtaking Olympic stadium, in the summer of 1992, it will mark the opening of the greatest sporting show on earth.

Held in Spain, the event will attract an audience of millions of TV viewers, and will generate enough money to run several small countries.

The Olympics have changed completely from the days when athletes were truly amateur. Some critics feel this has taken the greatness from the Games – they say that money, rather than just competing, has become important – while other critics say the Olympics are simply moving with the times.

It is true that the Games are very different from the concept that Baron Pierre de Coubertin created a hundred

In the early days of the Olympics, athletes trained hard for the Games just as they do today – their prize was an olive wreath.

years ago, when he decided to revive the Olympics. There had been a sporting occasion in Ancient Greece, held at a place called Olympia, every four years. These games at Olympia were a regular event from around 776 BC until they were banned by the Roman Emperor Theodosius in AD 393.

It was in the early 1890s that de Coubertin, inspired by stories from the ancient world and the sporting spirit of British public schools, decided to revive the Games. It took him three years to gain support but, eventually, he persuaded a wealthy Greek businessman to provide enough money to launch the first modern Olympics, in Athens, in 1896. De Coubertin's official motto for the Games was:

The important thing in the Olympic Games is not to win, but to take part, just as the important thing in life is not the triumph but the struggle; the essential thing is not to have conquered but to have fought well.

Baron Pierre de Coubertin broke with family tradition and gave up a career in the army to campaign for the Olympic movement.

The Olympic flame – the most stunning symbol of the spirit of the Games.

Since then, the Olympics have been held every four years and have grown in size and stature.

The symbols of the Games are the Olympic flame, carried by torch from Olympia, in Greece, to each Olympiad, and the Olympic flag, with its five interlocking coloured rings – blue, yellow, black, green and red. Every national flag in the world has at least one of these colours.

In Seoul, South Korea, in 1988, more than 13,800 athletes and officials came to the Games. The Games in Barcelona promise to be an even bigger occasion.

Basketball

Basketball is well known as one of the most popular professional sports in the USA. But the amateur Olympic competition has provided its own fair share of thrills, drama and controversy.

The tournaments are played on a group system, followed by quarter finals, semifinals and finals. The game is played by two teams of five players on an indoor court, as in the professional basketball leagues around the world.

The first Olympic basketball tournament was held at the 1936 Berlin Games on an outdoor tennis court. The USA team, from Universal Studios, had objected to a ruling that banned players over the height of 1.91 m – it would have lost them several key players. In fact, it was their 2.03 m centre, Joe Fortenberry, who scored half of the team's points in the final against Canada.

The USA went on to win every Olympic tournament, without losing a single game, until 1972 – an incredible winning streak lasting sixty-two games. They were defeated by the USSR in the 1972 final – a game which ended in controversy. The USSR currently holds the men's Olympic title, and basketball has grown into one of the nation's most popular sports.

Women's Olympic basketball began in 1976, in Montreal, and has been dominated by the USA, who are reigning champions, and the USSR.

The amazing game

One particular basketball match ranks as one of the most talked about events in Olympic history. It took place in the final at the 1972 Munich Games, between the USA and the USSR. Up to these Games, the USA had won every Olympic competition; but the Soviet team were playing well and had won every game on their way to the final.

There was just one second left on the clock when the USA took the lead, for the first time in the match, at 50–49. But the USSR claimed the referee had ignored their call for a time-out, and it was decided to set the clock back to show three seconds left. Incredibly, the USSR scored, just as the end-buzzer sounded, to win the title 51–50. The Americans were so angry that they refused to accept their silver medals.

Right *Action from the USA v USSR 1972 final.* **Opposite** *Seoul, 1988. Romania and the USSR battle it out.*

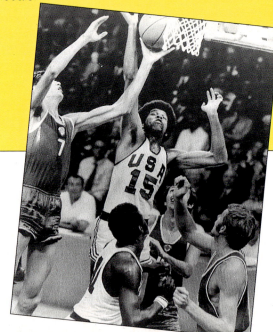

Boxing

Boxing was introduced at the 1904 Games, in St Louis, in the USA. The sport follows the strict amateur boxing code of three rounds of three minutes each and, today, all boxers must wear headguards.

The competition is for men only and is run on an elimination basis: the winner of the final takes the gold, the beaten finalist wins the silver and, since 1952, the two losing semifinalists both get bronze medals.

The current competition is contested in twelve weight divisions and, although no professionals are allowed in the Olympic competition, the Games are often seen as the starting point for many fine professional careers. The Olympics have launched no less than seven world heavyweight champions, including the legendary Muhammad Ali, Joe Frazier, George Foreman and Evander Holyfield, plus a variety of other world champions, including Alan Minter and Sugar Ray Leonard.

The current Olympic champions now starting professional careers, and tipped to be challenging for world titles, include light heavyweight Andrew Maynard, heavyweight Ray Mercer and super heavyweight Lennox Lewis.

One of the great stars of Olympic boxing is a Cuban, Teofilo Stevenson.

In his last Olympic final, Laszlo Papp beat American José Torres. Torres would go on to become world light heavyweight champion – a title Papp was never allowed to contest.

Laszlo Papp (Hungary)

Laszlo Papp is perhaps the most successful boxer in Olympic history. He won his first gold medal as a middleweight at the 1948 London Games, and then returned four years later, in Helsinki, to win the light middleweight title. To cap an amazing career, he then successfully defended his title in the 1956 Games in Melbourne.

A year later, at the age of thirty-one, he was given government permission to fight professionally – the first boxer from a communist country to do so. He won the European middleweight title but his government would not let him fight for the world title. He retired undefeated in 1965 and became coach to Hungary's Olympic boxing team.

Boxing weight divisions

light flyweight
flyweight
bantamweight
featherweight
lightweight
light welterweight
welterweight
light middleweight
middleweight
light heavyweight
heavyweight
super heavyweight

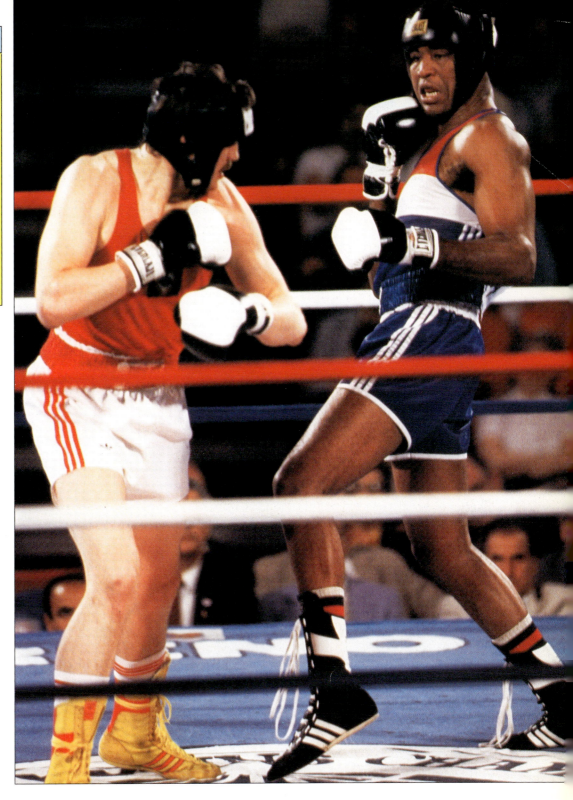

A handsome Cuban, Teofilo Stevenson was the most impressive Olympic boxer since the great Muhammad Ali.

Statues were erected in the Cuban capital Havana to mark his achievements in the Olympic ring.

He rejected every offer to turn professional. 'Professional boxing treats a fighter like a commodity,' he said, 'to be bought and sold and discarded when he is no longer of use.'

He has never fought as a professional. Many promoters have tried to tempt him with huge sums of money (including one offer of $2 million) to fight as a professional outside Cuba.

He won his first gold medal as a super heavyweight in Munich, in 1972, then won the same title in 1976 and 1980 – becoming the first man to win three golds in the same division.

Cycling

Cycling is one of the toughest events of the Olympic Games and demands incredible levels of training and physical fitness. Speeds of more than 65 kph have been reached.

There are two types of competition at the Games – track cycling and road cycling. In track cycling, the arena or velodrome is 333.33 m round, 7 m wide, and has high banks on the curves. The races are often tactical, with cyclists climbing the banks and waiting for each other to make a sprint for the finish line.

There are five men's track events: 1,000 m sprint, 1,000 m time trial, 4,000 m individual pursuit, 4,000 m team pursuit, and a 50 km race. On the road there are two men's events: 100 km team trial and a road race of

Seoul, 1988. The US 100 km team in the high-tech world of Olympic cycling.

about 197 km. Many cycling events have been discontinued down the years, including a twelve-hour race and a tandem event.

Women's cycling began with a single event at the 1984 Los Angeles Games – the road race. In 1988 in Seoul, the 1,000 m sprint was introduced.

France heads the overall men's cycling table, with a staggering sixty-two medals, twenty-seven of them gold. However, the USSR and East Germany have been the most powerful cycling nations at recent Olympics, but German reunification (see glossary) may change the dominance of Eastern European countries.

New lightweight cycles

Racing cycles have changed dramatically in recent years. A modern cycle weighs as little as 6.3 kg, and is made from lightweight metal alloys and carbon fibre. The carbon fibre disc wheels have silk-covered tyres, and are bigger at the rear to help with streamlining. To cut wind resistance, the riders wear silk clothes and shoes with no laces or buckles, just velcro straps. They wear aerodynamic helmets, made from toughened polystyrene.

Above *Bernd Dittart won a bronze medal in the 4,000 m Individual Pursuit for East Germany at Seoul's velodrome. Dittart was beaten by the eventual winner, Australia's Dean Woods, in the semi-finals.*

Decathlon/Heptathlon

The decathlon and heptathlon are arguably the toughest of all Olympic athletic events, requiring all-round fitness and ability. The Olympic champions are recognized as the world's finest athletes.

The decathlon includes ten events – four track and six field – contested by men over a two-day period. On the first day, the athletes must complete the 100 m, long jump, shot put, high jump and 400 m. On the second day, they complete the 110 m hurdles, discus, pole vault, javelin and 1500 m.

The heptathlon includes seven events – contested by women over two days. Heptathletes compete in the 100 m hurdles, shot put, high jump and 200 m on the first day. On the second day they contest the long jump, javelin and 800 m.

The decathlon first appeared in the Stockholm Olympics in 1912, and included the legendary American Jim Thorpe. He had taken part in three other events at the Games before entering the decathlon. But he won the competition by a huge margin and with a world record number of points.

The USA has won ten gold medals in

Daley Thompson (Great Britain)

Frances Morgan (Daley) Thompson exploded onto the decathlon scene at the tender age of just sixteen. A year later he finished eighteenth in the 1976 Olympics, but impressed the gold medal winner, Bruce Jenner, so much that he tipped him as his successor four years later in Moscow.

Thompson's fanatical training regime paid off handsomely in 1980, when he broke the world record in a pre-Olympic competition, and then comfortably took the gold medal in Moscow the same year. He sent a postcard to double gold medal winner Bob Mathias saying simply 'I'm going for three.'

He made it two gold medals in Los Angeles in 1984, with a world record performance, but an injury leading up to the Seoul Olympics in 1988 ended his chance of a unique treble.

Daley Thompson – seen here training for the discus throw.

Jackie Joyner-Kersee's world record *(Seoul, 1988)*

Day one	100 m hurdles	12.60 sec
	Shot put	15.8 m
	High jump	1.86 m
	200 m	22.56 sec
Day two	Long jump	7.27 m
	Javelin	45.66 m
	800 m	2 min 8.51 sec
Total points		7,291

the decathlon with sporting greats such as Bob Mathias, who won the decathlon in 1948 when he was just seventeen, and went on to win it in 1952. However, the USA has not claimed a gold medal in the decathlon since Bruce Jenner's gold medal at the Montreal Games of 1976.

The 1988 decathlon champion was Germany's Christian Schenk, beating the winner of the previous two decathlons – Daley Thompson.

The heptathlon first became an Olympic event at the 1984 Los Angeles Games, replacing the five-event pentathlon. USA's Jackie Joyner-Kersee just missed gold in Los Angeles by five points, losing to Australian Glynnis Nunn. However, Joyner-Kersee came back in 1988 at Seoul to take the Olympic title and world record as well as the individual gold medal in the long jump.

Jackie Joyner-Kersee during the shot put section of the heptathlon competition. Rigorous training produced a series of outstanding results in all seven events.

Distance running

Long distance races are some of the biggest events at the Olympics. The events we know today – the 5,000 m and 10,000 m – were first staged at the 1912 Games, in Stockholm.

Before 1912 there was an odd collection of races, such as the 5 miles (8,046 m), 12,000 m cross-country and 4 mile (6,437 m) team race. However, after the Paris Games of 1924, only the track races at 5,000 m and 10,000 m remained.

Paavo Nurmi (Finland)

Paavo Nurmi ran his last Olympic race more than sixty years ago, but he still stands out as one of the giants of the Games. He won an incredible nine gold medals at three Olympics in the 1920s, and created an astonishing twenty-nine world records during his career.

He probably would have ended his career at the 1932 Los Angeles Olympics with a gold in the marathon, but he was disqualified a week before the race for accepting expenses for an exhibition tour. An impressive statue of him now stands outside Helsinki's Olympic stadium.

Seoul, 1988. The USSR's powerful Olga Bondarenko won the first ever Olympic 10,000 m for women in 31 min 5.21 sec.

Nurmi – king of distance running.

Nurmi's medal chart

	1920	1924	1928
1,500 m		gold	
5,000 m	silver	gold	silver
10,000 m		gold	gold
3,000 m steeplechase			silver
Cross-country	gold	gold	
3,000 m team		gold	
Cross-country team	gold	gold	

Total = 9 gold, 3 silver

For the women, the Soviets dominated the Seoul Games, with Tatiana Samolenko winning the 3,000 m and Olga Bondarenko winning the 10,000 m.

The 5,000 m is twelve-and-a-half laps of the track, and fifteen athletes contest the Olympic final. The 10,000 m is twenty-five laps of the track, and twenty athletes run in the Olympic final.

Until recently, long distance events were considered to be too tough for women. But this view has been proved wrong, and at the 1984 Los Angeles Games the 3,000 m for women was introduced, followed in 1988 in Seoul by the introduction of the 10,000 m.

The early Olympics were dominated by the Finns, particularly Paavo Nurmi, arguably the greatest long distance runner of all time.

In the 1950s, he was matched by the legendary Czech, Emil Zatopek, and then by the USSR's Vladimir Kuts. In the 1970s, the Finns had double Olympic champion, Lasse Viren. The current Olympic champions are Kenya's John Ngugi, in the 5,000 m, and Morocco's Brahim Boutaib, in the 10,000 m.

Kenya's John Ngugi wins in the 5,000 m in Seoul. His time – 13 min 11.07 sec.

Equestrian events

Horse riding events were not included in the first Olympics, but appeared at the next Games, in Paris, in 1900. There were only three events: showjumping, high jump and long jump.

Equestrian events were then dropped from the Games until the 1912 Olympics, in Stockholm, when further events were added, though the high jump and long jump were discarded.

Today, there are six equestrian events, and they are the only Olympic events in which men and women compete together. There are the team and individual events in jumping, dressage, and the three-day event. In jumping, or *prix des nations*, horse and rider must negotiate a series of

Three-day eventing can be hazardous – especially over the water jump!

obstacles in as fast a time as possible. Points, or faults, are added for mistakes, and the riders and teams with the least points win the competition.

In dressage, riders must put their horses through a series of movements, which show the level of control and communication between them. Points are awarded for how well each movement is completed.

Jumping and dressage form the first two-thirds of the three-day event.

Mark Todd (New Zealand)

Mark Todd is widely considered to be the world's best horseman. His horse, Charisma, is also regarded as one of the greatest mounts ever to appear in an Olympic competition.

Todd, a dairy farmer, sold most of his herd to pay for the preparation needed to take part in the Olympics. He and Charisma carried off the individual three-day event title at the 1984 Los Angeles Games, and then repeated the feat in Seoul four years later.

The greatest double act in Olympic equestrianism – Todd and Charisma.

The grace and style of the 1988 Olympic dressage final, in Seoul – a competition dominated and won by West Germany.

The final part is a long distance event. This is broken into four sections – two sets of road and track; a steeplechase and a cross-country. Penalty points are deducted for mistakes, but bonus points are awarded for completing any of the four sections of the course within the time limit.

Before reunification West Germany had the best medal record, with a total of fifty-seven medals, including the team title at the three-day event, at the 1988 Seoul Olympics.

Gymnastics

Gymnastics is one of the most popular Olympic events and has evolved into today's competition from a wide variety of floor and apparatus exercises.

The men's competition began at the 1900 Paris Games and included no less than eleven different disciplines, including heaving a 50 kg stone and rope climbing. The women's competition did not start until the 1952 Helsinki Olympics.

Today, the gymnastics competition is divided into three parts. On the first two days, each competitor performs on all the apparatus. For men this includes the horizontal bar, parallel bar, long-horsed vault, pommel horse, rings and floor exercises.

Olympic gymnastic goddess Olga Korbut.

Olga Korbut (USSR)

Olga Korbut, probably the most famous gymnast of all time, actually finished seventh in the all-round competition at the 1972 Munich Olympics. It was won by another Soviet, nineteen-year-old Lyudmila Tourischeva with one of the truly outstanding Olympic gymnastic performances. Yet the world was enthralled by the seventeen-year-old from Grodno, in Byelorussia. Korbut was actually a reserve for the Soviet team and only made the competition because a team-mate was injured.

Korbut performed well at the start of the all-round competition, but then she slipped and fell from the asymmetrical bars. But she returned to win two individual gold medals, with dazzling performances on the beam and the floor.

Above Sweden's Johan Jonasson demonstrates the strength and balance required in the men's horizontal bars.

For women, there are the horse vault, asymmetrical bars, beam and floor exercises.

Once the winners of the team event are decided, the thirty-six gymnasts with the highest scores go forward to the individual, all-round final in which they compete on all the apparatus for a second time. Those with the top eight scores in the all-round final then go on to the individual apparatus finals.

The men's event has been dominated by Eastern Europe, particularly the Soviet Union, where standards of strength and fitness are exceptional.

But it is the women's event that has produced the star names, such as Soviet champions Vera Caslavska, Lyudmila Tourischeva, and reigning champion Elena Chouchounova.

But the biggest name of all did not win an all-round title. Olga Korbut won just two individual exercises in Munich, in 1972, but captured the hearts of television viewers around the world with her charm and humour.

Elena Chouchounova accepts the applause of the Seoul crowd after taking her gold medal as all-round women's gymnastic champion.

High jump

The high jump competition at the 1968 Mexico City Olympics marked the end of one era and the start of a new one. And the man who was responsible for the change was an American, Dick Fosbury.

Until then, the high jump had been contested in much the same style. Competitors would often use the straddle technique, where the athlete jumps, swings a leg over the bar and passes face down over it. In fact, a high jumper is allowed to clear the bar in any way he or she chooses, except that the take-off must be on one foot.

In Mexico City, Fosbury left the Olympic crowd, and millions of television viewers, completely stunned. He ran at the bar and then, instead of lifting a leg, he jumped backwards over the bar. His unique technique instantly became known as the Fosbury flop, and it enabled Fosbury to win the gold medal. Within ten years the vast majority of high jumpers were using this technique.

Down the years, the high jump record has improved steadily. The 2 m barrier was cleared in 1912, now 2 m 50 cm is the target.

The start of an athletic revolution – Dick Fosbury flops over the bar to win the gold medal and change high jumping for ever.

High jump world records

Men	
1912	2.00m
1941	2.10m
1960	2.22m
1973	2.30m
1980	2.35m
1985	2.40m
1989	2.44m

Women	
1924	1.51m
1928	1.60m
1943	1.71m
1958	1.80m
1961	1.90m
1977	2.00m
1987	2.09m

Louise Ritter (USA)

After finishing a disappointing eighth at the 1984 Los Angeles Olympics, the high jump career of USA's Louise Ritter quite literally took off.

Despite winning countless USA titles, her only major international success was a bronze medal at the 1983 World Championships, in Helsinki.

Few people thought the thirty-year-old Ritter had much chance of winning at Seoul, particularly against Bulgaria's young world record holder, Stefka Kostadinova. But her experience helped her to break the Olympic record with a leap of 2.03 m.

Kostadinova could not repeat her prodigious world record, of 2.09 m, set in 1987, and an elated Ritter took the gold.

The reigning men's Olympic champion is Guennadi Avdeenko, of the USSR, while in the women's competition the current champion is USA's Louise Ritter.

Despite this 1987 Grand Prix success in Zurich, where she jumped 2.04 m, many felt Ritter was past her best before Seoul!

Hurdles

Hurdling is widely regarded as one of the most skilful events of track and field athletics. It demands a mixture of speed, balance and extraordinary concentration and technique.

Harrison Dillard, the only man ever to win Olympic titles at 100 m and 110 m hurdles, maintains that hurdling represents a far tougher challenge than sprinting: 'When you run the hurdles there are ten obstacles to negotiate cleanly and clearly – that's ten opportunities to fail.'

For men, there are two kinds of hurdling – 110 m high hurdles and 400 m hurdles. In the 110 m hurdles there are ten flights of 1.07 m to jump; while the 400 m has ten 91.4 cm barriers.

For women the high hurdles race is run over 100 m, with ten 83.8 cm barriers; while the 400 m hurdles, only introduced at the Los Angeles Games in 1984, is run over ten flights of 76.2 cm.

European record holder Colin Jackson won silver in the Seoul 110 m hurdles. The young Welshman may be favourite in 1992.

Edwin Moses (USA)

Ed Moses, twice Olympic champion and world record holder for the 400 m hurdles since 1983, is probably the greatest hurdler of all time.

His reign as the undisputed hurdles king and one of track's great stars began at the 1976 Olympics when, at just twenty, he took the gold medal in world record time. He put together an unbelievable winning streak that lasted 107 races and nearly ten years.

Moses missed the 1980 Moscow Olympics because the USA refused to go in protest against the USSR's invasion of Afghanistan. However, it is almost certain he would have won, and he returned to win in Los Angeles in 1984.

He bettered his own world record three more times to 47.02 sec, and even managed to take a bronze medal at the Seoul Games of 1988, at the age of thirty-three, before announcing his retirement.

The men's 110 m hurdles is currently dominated by USA's Roger Kingdom, the world record holder, at 12.92 sec, and Olympic champion in both 1984 and 1988. But Britain's Colin Jackson, silver medallist in Seoul in 1988, is younger and getting faster.

The women's event has seen a battle between the powerful East European athletes. The current Olympic champion and record holder is Bulgaria's Yordanka Donkova, in 12.38 sec.

The 400 m event is known in athletics as the 'man killer' because it is so physically demanding. Since 1983, hurdlers have been chasing the world record of USA's Ed Moses, set at 47.02 sec.

The women's 400 m event was run for the first time in 1984. It produced a thrilling race in the 1988 final with Australia's Debbie Flintoff-King winning by 100th of a second, with the time of 53.17 sec, from the USSR's Tatyana Ledovskaya.

Ed Moses, one of track and fields' great ambassadors, after his 1984 400 m hurdles victory in Los Angeles. He also won in 1976.

Javelin

The javelin throw is one of the few field events that can be traced back to the ancient Olympics. Yet it was not included in the first modern Games held in Athens in 1896.

The javelin throw was first staged at the 1908 London Olympics, and it was then dominated by throwers from the Scandinavian countries, with Finland and Sweden sharing the title in the next six Olympiads.

Although the Scandinavian countries no longer win every competition, they still produce great throwers and maintain a strong javelin tradition.

The javelin must weigh a minimum of 800 g and measure between 2.60 and 2.70 m. It can be made from wood or metal, and must be thrown on the run from above the shoulder. To count as a legitimate throw, the athlete must not cross the throwing line, and the tip of the javelin must mark the ground when it lands.

In 1986, modifications to the men's javelin were made to reduce the distances they could be thrown. Officials were worried about the safety of runners on the track and spectators on the far side of stadia, because the javelins were being thrown so far.

Below *The arrows mark the points of javelin world records.*

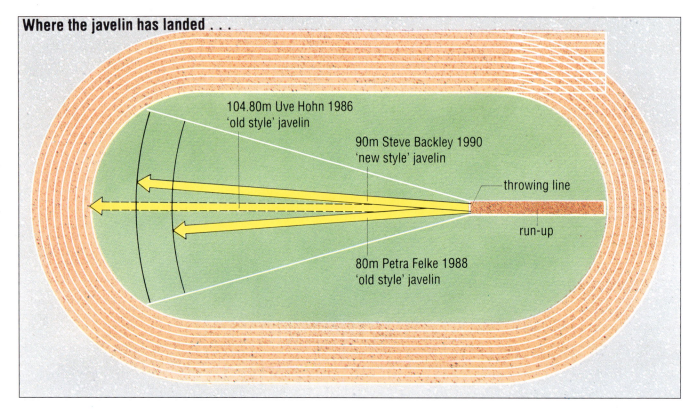

Above *Britain's javelin world record holder Steve Backley shows the power which makes him the runaway favourite for a gold medal in the 1992 Barcelona Olympics.*

The men's world record with the 'old style' javelin had reached 104.80 m, held by Uwe Hohn (then competing for East Germany). In the women's event, Germany's reigning Olympic champion, Petra Felke, holds the world record at exactly 80 m.

The 1988 men's Olympic champion was Finland's Tapio Korjus. Meanwhile Britain's Steve Backley, who became the first man to throw over 90 m with the 'new style' javelin in 1990, looks as if he will be the man to beat in the Games in 1992.

Petra Felke (Germany)

Germany's Petra Felke was first noticed as a top javelin thrower in 1981, when she won titles in both the World Student Games and the World Cup. But it was in 1985, when she set two world records in the same competition, that she became the outstanding thrower.

Just before the 1988 Seoul Olympics, she became the first woman to throw 80 m and, less than a month later, became the Olympic champion and record holder, beating her great rival, Britain's Fatima Whitbread, with a throw of 74.68 m.

Felke competed for East Germany until 1990, when East and West Germany were reunified. She could be the last in a line of great East German javelin throwers, a list that includes her idol, the double Olympic champion, Ruth Fuchs. The reunification of Germany has meant the break-up of the East German powerful state-funded sports network. Petra Felke's coach was one of the first to be made unemployed.

Petra Felke – one of the great Olympic competitors – seen here at Seoul.

Judo

Judo was developed from various forms of the martial art, ju-jitsu, by the Japanese unarmed combat master, Dr Jigoro Kano, in the nineteenth century.

He founded the first judo school, and when his techniques were shown outside of Japan, the sport began to grow in popularity.

It was fitting that when judo became an Olympic sport, its first appearance was at the 1964 Toyko Games. Women's judo, which was only a demonstration sport at the 1988 Olympics in Seoul, will be included as a full sport in Barcelona.

There are seven weight categories in the men's competition – extra lightweight, half lightweight, lightweight, half middleweight, middleweight, half heavyweight and heavyweight.

A judo match is won by throwing an opponent cleanly on to his or her back or holding him or her there for 30 seconds. A win can also be achieved by forcing a submission from an arm lock or a stranglehold, or from a decision by two judges and the referee.

All the contests in each weight category take place on the same day,

The final of the demonstration women's judo at Seoul. Britain's world champion Diane Bell (right) beat the USA's Lynn Roethke.

and each bout is allowed five minutes.

Japan, perhaps understandably, has the best Olympic record with twenty-two medals, fourteen of them gold. But in recent years, the rest of the world has caught up with the sport that Japan created, and the medals have been much more evenly spread.

Yasuhiro Yamashita (Japan)

One of the most fearsome men of the judo world was Japan's enormous heavyweight, Yasuhiro Yamashita. As a young man, Yamashita was beaten in the 1977 Japanese Student Championships final. He vowed never to lose again, and for seven years he kept his word. He was unbeaten at all levels for 194 matches.

One opponent described the giant Yamashita as a 'fridge with a head on top'. His dream was an Olympic gold medal, but when Japan joined the boycott of the 1980 Moscow Games, he had to wait until the 1984 Los Angeles Games before his dream finally came true.

Left *Japan's Yasuhiro Yamashita. When Japan joined the 1980 Olympic boycott, Yamashita appeared on TV in tears to try and get the decision reversed!*

Below *Japan's Akinobu Osako, bronze medallist in Seoul, throws Brazil's Walter Carmona.*

Long jump

This event has been dominated by one man for more than twenty years: USA's Bob Beamon. His jump has been replayed thousands of times on TV, and is the longest surviving world record.

At the 1968 Mexico City Olympics, Beamon leaped into sporting history. His record-shattering mark of 8 m 90 cm has frustrated long jumpers ever since.

After the distance had been announced, the reigning Olympic champion, Britain's Lynn Davies, went over to him and said simply, 'You have destroyed this event.'

Men's long jumping began at the first Olympics, while women's long jumping began at the London Olympics, in 1948.

Athletes must have good running speed and a proficient jumping technique. Speed is needed on the runway, and a good technique is needed to get height and distance on the jump. This combination makes it a spectacular event to watch, and it has become one of the most popular of the field events.

There is a take-off board and an athlete must not step over the edge nearest the sand pit or his or her effort will be declared a 'no jump'. The edge is marked with soft plastic, and the slightest impression is easily seen. The measurement of a jump is taken from the take-off board to the nearest mark made by any part of the athlete's body in the sand pit.

Probably the athletic feat of the century. Bob Beamon destroys the world long jump record by an astonishing 55 cm in Mexico.

The current Olympic champion is USA's Carl Lewis, who won in Seoul, in 1988, with a leap of 8 m 72 cm. He also won in 1984 in Los Angeles. He is determined to be the first nine-metre jumper.

The current women's Olympic champion is USA's Jackie Joyner-Kersee. The women's world record of 7 m 52 cm is held by USSR's Galina Chistyakova.

Long jump world records (in metres)			
Men		Women (major landmarks)	
1901	7.60	1922	5.16
1921	7.69	1926	5.50
1924	7.76	1928	5.98
1925	7.89	1939	6.12
1928	7.93	1943	6.25
1931	7.98	1962	6.53
1935	8.13	1970	6.84
1960	8.21	1976	6.99
1961	8.28	1978	7.09
1962	8.31	1982	7.20
1964	8.34	1983	7.43
1965	8.35	1986	7.45
1968	8.90	1988	7.52

The great US long jumper and heptathlete Jackie Joyner-Kersee leaps to another gold.

This drawing shows just how far the long jump record has progressed.

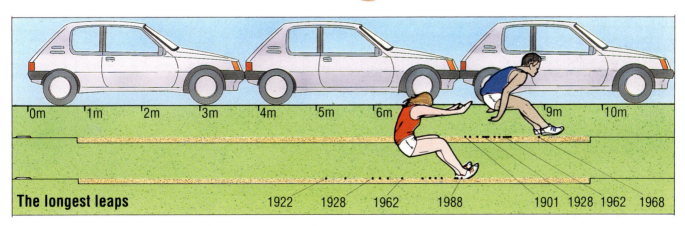

The longest leaps

29

Marathon

Only one of today's races dates back to the ancient Olympics. That race is the marathon and no other running event has provided so much drama.

The legend dates back to 490 BC and tells of a Greek soldier who carried news of a great victory at the battlefield of Marathon to Athens – a distance of 26 miles (41.8 km).

When the modern Olympics began in Athens, in 1896, the marathon was the most eagerly awaited event. Seventeen athletes, all but four of them Greek, took part in the race, and it was won by a local shepherd called Spiridon Louis, who was presented with his medal and a horse and cart for his village.

The marathon grew in popularity around the world and, at the London Olympics of 1908, it was decided the race would be run from Windsor Castle to the stadium at White City, in West London. That was exactly 26 miles 385 yards (42.2 km), and since

Dorando Pietri is helped to the finish line only to be disqualified.

then this unusual distance has been the official marathon distance. Today, the race is started in the stadium, then winds around the Olympic city and finishes back in the stadium. It remained a men's event until the 1984 Los Angeles Olympics, when the first women's marathon was run.

This event has been won by a wide variety of nationalities and has given us some extraordinary tales. For example, at the 1908 London Games, the leader, Italy's Dorando Pietri, came staggering into the stadium only to be helped across the finish line by officials – he was then disqualified for not running the whole race unaided.

Only two men have won the Olympic title twice – the bare-footed Ethiopian Abebe Bikela (1960, 1964), and East Germany's Waldemar Cierpinski (1976, 1980). The current men's champion is Italy's Gelindo Bordin, and the reigning women's champion is Portugal's Rosa Mota.

Rosa Mota (Portugal)

When Rosa Mota took her third European marathon title at the 1990 European games in Split, Yugoslavia, she confirmed her status as one of the great female marathon runners.

The world record, held by Norway's Ingrid Kristiansen, set in 1985 at 2 hr 21 min 6 sec, is now Mota's target.

Mota beat Kristiansen in the 1984 Olympic marathon, but only finished with a bronze medal. She became the first Portuguese woman to win an Olympic medal.

In 1988 in Seoul, she destroyed a world-class field to win the Olympic title, but finished nearly six minutes outside Kristiansen's world record. Mota now wants to become the first woman to retain an Olympic marathon title.

Men's Olympic winning times

	Hr	Min	Sec				
1896	2	58	50	1952	2	23	03
1900	2	59	45	1956	2	25	00
1904	3	28	53	1960	2	15	16
1908	2	55	18	1964	2	12	11
1912	2	36	54	1968	2	20	26
1920	2	32	35	1972	2	12	19
1924	2	41	22	1976	2	09	55
1928	2	32	57	1980	2	11	03
1932	2	31	36	1984	2	09	21
1936	2	29	19				
1948	2	34	51				

Portugal's marathon queen Rosa Mota shows the strain of winning the title in Seoul.

Middle-distance running

The appeal of the two middle-distance events – the 800 m and 1500 m – never wanes. These events have produced some memorable races and personalities over the years.

Gold medal winners in the men's 800 m include such stars as Peter Snell, Alberto Juantorena and Steve Ovett; while in the 1500 m there have been the likes of Paavo Nurmi, Jack Lovelock, Herb Elliott and Sebastian Coe.

The women's 800 m was run only once before 1960, and is now dominated by Eastern Europe. The current Olympic champion is Germany's Sigrun Wodars, but the world record holder is Czechoslovakia's Jarmila Kratochvilova, whose time of 1 min 53.28 sec was set in 1983. The 1500 m for women was first staged at the 1972 Munich Games, and the great Romanian Paula Ivan is the reigning champion.

The 800 m is started in eight staggered lanes, and the athletes

Kenya's Peter Rono wins the men's 1500 m in Seoul – a fraction ahead of Britain's Peter Elliott.

Paula Ivan (Romania)

Romania's powerful athlete Paula Ivan has dominated the women's 1500 m event for the last three years. Despite the number of talented athletes around the world there seems to be no-one who can challenge her. She took the Olympic 1500 m title at Seoul in a new Olympic record time of 3 min 53.96 sec. But it was a second-and-a-half slower than the 3 m 52.4 sec world record time of Tatyana Kazankina, from the USSR.

Ivan has her sights set on that 1500 m world record, set back in 1980, and has already shown she has the ability to break it. In July 1989, she smashed the world mile (1609 m) record, in Nice, with a time of 4 min 15.61 sec. Although a woman breaking the four-minute-mile barrier is a long way off, Ivan is making great strides towards it.

The relentless power of Romania's amazing Paula Ivan – the world mile record holder.

'break' for the inside lane when they reach the back straight for the first time. The current men's Olympic champion is Kenya's Paul Ereng, while the world record still stands to Britain's Sebastian Coe, whose time of 1 min 41.73 sec was set in June 1981.

The 1500 m is started on a curved line across the track, and all the athletes break for the inside lane as soon as the gun goes off. The reigning men's Olympic champion is another Kenyan, Peter Rono, while Morocco's Said Aouita holds the world record at 3 min 29.46 sec, which he set in 1985.

Moscow, 1980. The face of Britain's great middle-distance runner Sebastian Coe tells the story. After losing to rival Steve Ovett in the 800 m, he returns to win the 1500 m.

Modern pentathlon

Modern pentathlon, though it sounds like a new event, actually began at the 1912 Stockholm Olympics. Five events are contested – horse riding, fencing, shooting, swimming and running.

This all-male event is based on the idea that the athlete is a soldier with orders to deliver a message. He starts out on horseback, has to fight a duel with swords, is then trapped and has to shoot his way out with pistols. He swims across a river and finally delivers his message by running through the woods.

Modern pentathlon, which requires stamina, skill and bravery, comprises one event each day for five days.

First, there is a horse riding course with fifteen obstacles to jump; then fencing with an electric épée; a 300 m freestyle swimming course; then pistol

Fencing during the Seoul modern penthathlon competition. This photographic impression shows the agility required.

34

Olympic scandal

Modern pentathlon suffered one of the biggest Olympic scandals at the Montreal Games, in 1976. The USSR's Boris Onishenko, an army major who had won a gold and two silver medals in the event at the previous two Olympics, was found to be cheating. In the fencing competition it was discovered that he had wired his electric épée to 'beep' even when he had not scored a hit. Onishenko was disqualified and sent home in disgrace. He has never been seen outside the USSR since.

Above *A Montreal judge examines the épée of USSR's Boris Onishenko.*

Britain's Dominic Mahony, a team bronze medallist in Seoul, fights his way through the modern pentathlon cross-country course.

shooting at targets at a distance of 25 m; ending with a 4,000 m cross-country run.

There is an individual competition and, since 1952, a team event. The scoring is done on a points basis. The better the performance in each event, the more points the athlete gets.

Sweden lost only one of the first nine individual Olympic titles, but they have not won the event since 1968. The reigning Olympic champion is Hungary's Janos Martenek, who also won the gold medal as part of his country's three-man winning team.

Pole vault

Pole vaulting is one of the world's oldest field events – it was even practised by King Henry VIII! In simple terms, the athlete sprints down a runway and vaults over a high bar with the aid of a pole.

Until early this century, the poles were made from wood, but these were very heavy and were replaced by more flexible bamboo poles. The aluminium pole arrived in the 1950s, followed a few years later by the lighter and extremely flexible fibreglass poles that are still used today. The vaulters have the added assistance of a 'box' into which the pole is pushed when attempting a vault.

Pole vaulting was included at the very first Games in Athens, in 1896. The winning vault on that occasion was 3 m 30 cm, by USA's Bill Hoyt. The USA then continued to win every Olympic pole vault competition until 1972, when East Germany's Wolfgang Nordwig took the gold medal at the Munich Games. His winning vault was 5 m 50 cm.

Probably the most famous Olympic pole vaulter was USA's Bob Richards,

Pole vault Olympic records	
1896	3.30 m Bill Hoyt (USA)
1904	3.50 m Charles Dvorak (USA)
1908	3.71 m Edward Cooke (USA)
1912	3.95 m Harry Babcock (USA)
1920	4.09 m Frank Foss (USA)
1928	4.20 m Sabin Carr (USA)
1932	4.31 m Bill Miller (USA)
1936	4.35 m Earle Meadows (USA)
1952	4.55 m Bob Richards (USA)
1956	4.56 m Bob Richards (USA)
1960	4.70 m Don Bragg (USA)
1964	5.10 m Frederick Hansen (USA)
1968	5.40 m Bob Seagren (USA)
1972	5.50 m Wolfgang Nordwig (East Germany)
1980	5.78 m Wladislaw Kozakiewicz (Poland)
1988	5.90 m Sergey Bubka (USSR)

Paris, 1924. Olympic pole vaulting with a bamboo pole and a not-so-soft sandy landing.

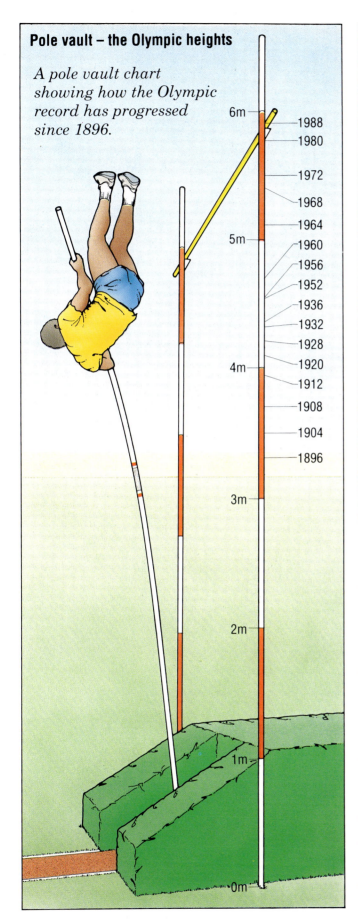

Pole vault – the Olympic heights

A pole vault chart showing how the Olympic record has progressed since 1896.

Sergey Bubka shows the power and strength that has made him the world record holder and reigning Olympic pole vault champion.

who won in 1952 and 1956. Reverend Richards was a professor of religious studies in California and became known as 'the vaulting vicar'.

The current world record holder and reigning Olympic champion is the amazing Sergey Bubka, of the USSR. He was the first man to vault 6 m, in 1986, and has since improved his own indoor world record to an astonishing 6 m 11 cm. In the world of track and field athletics, few athletes are described as invincible. Sergey Bubka is one of the few.

Rowing

Rowing was first staged at the 1900 Paris Games with four events. Today, men's rowing has eight events held over a 2,000 m course, while the six women's events are contested over a 1,000 m course.

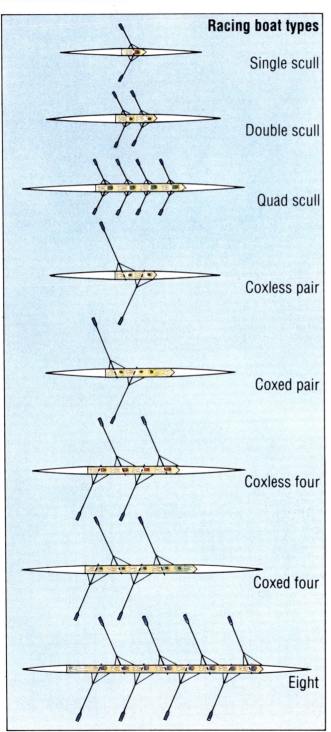

Racing boat types
- Single scull
- Double scull
- Quad scull
- Coxless pair
- Coxed pair
- Coxless four
- Coxed four
- Eight

In 1900, the men's event included the single sculls, coxed pairs, coxed fours, and the eights. Today, they have been joined by a further four events – the double sculls, quadruple sculls, coxless pairs and the coxless fours.

The difference between the rowing events, apart from the numbers, is whether or not there is a coxswain. He or she controls the speed and direction of the boat.

Women's rowing did not begin until the 1976 Montreal Olympics, and includes the single and double sculls, coxed quadruple sculls, coxless pairs, coxed fours and the eights.

Since the 1964 Tokyo Games, all rowing events begin with a qualifying series of races. The fastest eight qualifiers go automatically into the semifinals, while the 'eliminated' crews race again in *repêchages,* which give them another chance to qualify for the semifinals.

The four fastest crews from these *repêchages* then join the other semifinalists. The top six from the semifinals then contest the final.

Eastern Europe was a dominant force in men's Olympic rowing, particularly the USSR and East Germany, while Romania has been the source of some of the greatest women rowers to compete in the Olympics.

After the political changes in the late 1980s and early 1990s – in particular, the reunification of Germany – it will be interesting to see if Eastern Europe can maintain its grip on this event.

Vyacheslav Ivanov (USSR)

One of the most successful Olympic oarsmen is USSR's amazing Vyacheslav Ivanov. He won his first gold medal, in the single sculls, at the Melbourne Olympics, in 1956. Just eighteen years old, he was so thrilled about his victory he jumped up and down on the quayside winner's rostrum and his medal dropped into the lake. He promptly dived in to rescue it, but came up empty handed.

After the 1956 Games Ivanov was presented with a replacement medal. With his incredible finishing speed, Ivanov went on to win the same event at the next two Olympics. On both those occasions he managed to hold onto the medal!

Below *The members of the West German women's coxed four show the relief and delight of winning the gold medal at the 1988 Seoul Games.*

Above *The winner of the single sculls race in Rome, 1960. This time Vyacheslav Ivanov celebrates with the gold medal safely around his neck!*

Sprinting

One of the most exciting track events at the Olympic Games is the 100 m. It is a race that will decide who is the world's fastest man and fastest woman.

It is also an event that has produced some memorable performances. For instance, from athletes such as Britain's Harold Abrahams, who was portrayed in the film *Chariots of Fire,* and the legendary Jesse Owens and reigning Olympic champion Carl Lewis, both from the USA.

Women did not start competing in the Olympic sprints until 1928. It was one of the first events they were allowed to contest.

Eight men and women contest the finals and, since 1948, starting blocks have been used to give the sprinters a firmer and faster start.

In the days when athletes ran on cinder tracks, times were recorded using the hand-held stopwatch. Today, high-tech electronic timing is used, which can separate athletes to thousandths of a second as they hit the finish line on the super-fast synthetic tracks.

The USA won the first men's 100 m in Athens in 1896. Since then they have won the title no less than fourteen times from a total of twenty-one Olympiads.

At the 1988 Seoul Games, the competition ended in scandal when Canada's Ben Johnson was found to have taken performance-improving drugs and was disqualified, despite winning the final and breaking the world record. Second placed Carl Lewis was awarded the gold medal, becoming the first man to retain the title, and in the following year his

Seoul, 1988. The most infamous race in Olympic history. Ben Johnson smashed the 100 m world record in a time of 9.79 sec, beating Carl Lewis and Linford Christie. Then a routine drug test finds traces of steroid drugs in his body and he is disqualified.

time of 9.92 sec was confirmed as the new world record.

In Seoul, the women's sprints were completely dominated by USA's world record holder 'Flo-Jo', Florence Griffith-Joyner, who took the gold medal not only in the 100 m, but in the 200 m, and sprint relay as well, and then won a silver medal in the 4 × 400 m relay.

Jesse Owens (USA)

When the world's fastest men are asked to select their number one sprinter, the name is usually the same, Jesse Owens.

Owens, the youngest of ten children, was born into a poor Alabama family in 1913. It was not until he moved north to Cleveland, Ohio, that his amazing athletic ability was discovered. At just twenty-one, at a college meeting, he created a piece of track and field history by breaking five world records and equalling a sixth – all in the space of 45 minutes. The following year, in front of Adolf Hitler at the 1936 Berlin Olympics, he collected four gold medals for 100 m, 200 m, long jump, and 4 × 100 m relay.

Above *Despite winning four golds in Berlin, Jesse Owens was banned from racing by the USA in 1936 for refusing to run in Sweden.*

Left *The incredible 'Flo-Jo', USA's Florence Griffith-Joyner, wins another gold in Seoul.*

Swimming

The men's Olympic swimming competition took place at the first Games in 1896, in the open water of the Bay of Zea, near the Greek port of Piraeus.

The weather was cold and the swimmers had to brave icy water in the three Olympic events. Two were won by thirteen-year-old Hungarian Alfred Hajos, who took up swimming after his father had drowned.

More events were added over the years and today there are sixteen men's events, including individual races in freestyle, backstroke, breaststroke, butterfly and a medley of all four strokes. There are also three relays.

Women's events were introduced in 1912 and are similar to the men's, except they have an 800 m freestyle race, where the men's is 1500 m. The men also compete in an extra (4 × 200 m) relay race.

There have been many Olympic swimming stars over the years, including Duke Kahanamoku, a member of the Hawaiian royal family, who won three gold medals and a silver medal for the USA in the 1920 Olympics in Antwerp.

He was followed by the legendary Johnny Weissmuller, who won three gold medals for the USA at the 1924 Olympics, and two more in 1928. He then became even more famous as a movie star in Hollywood, playing Tarzan in more than a dozen films.

In women's swimming there were just as many stars, including multi-world record holder and 1932 gold medallist Eleanor Holm. She also became a Hollywood star but is best known for being suspended from the

The start of an Olympic backstroke final and the swimmers arch backwards for maximum lift and drive. The 1988 100 m champion was Japan's Daichi Suzuki, in a time of 55.05 sec.

Dawn Fraser (Australia)

Dawn Fraser won her first Olympic gold medal in her native Australia at the 1956 Melbourne Games, and broke the world record into the bargain. She was to hold the record, improving it consistently, for an astonishing fifteen years.

In 1962 she became the first woman to break the fabled minute barrier for the 100 m freestyle in 59.9 sec. Two years later she improved it to 58.9 sec. A month after setting this new world record she was badly injured in a car crash, in which her mother died. She had her neck in plaster for six weeks, but miraculously returned to win her third gold medal at the 1964 Tokyo Games.

Sadly, soon after her success, Dawn was in trouble with the Olympic officials. She had led a souvenir-raiding party on the Japanese Emperor's Palace to steal a flag. For this prank she was suspended by the Australian Swimming Union for ten years.

Above *Australia's medal-winning swimmer Dawn Fraser – 4 gold and 2 silver medals.*

USA team, just before the 1936 Berlin Olympics, for being drunk on board the team ship.

Arguably the greatest ever Olympic swimmer is the USA's Mark Spitz.

At the 1972 Munich Olympics he astounded everyone by winning an astonishing seven gold medals – a record number of victories in any sport at a single Games.

Today's Olympic stars include Kristin Otto who won six gold medals for East Germany at Seoul in 1988, and USA's Matt Biondi who won five gold medals, a silver and a bronze – also at Seoul.

Mark Spitz on his way to gold and another world record in the 100 m butterfly in Munich. Spitz was a star attraction for sponsorship and it made him a millionaire.

Carrying the flame

It is difficult to know what Baron de Coubertin, the founder of the modern Olympic movement, would think about the Olympic Games if he were alive today.

It is possible he would feel they have moved away from the pure sporting games he had dreamed about. But it is also possible he would feel that they reflect today's ideals.

What is certain is that the Olympic movement is stronger than ever, and the Games remain the greatest sporting festival in the world. The Games are attended by the best athletes and, through TV, the Olympics are watched by more people than any other sporting event.

In Barcelona, three new sports will join the Olympic list – women's judo, baseball and badminton. There will also be three demonstration sports: the martial art taekwondo, roller-hockey and pelota, a ball game played by two players, and said to be the 'fastest game in the world'.

The number of Olympic sports will rise to an impressive twenty-eight, and will include, apart from the sports already mentioned: archery, canoeing, diving, fencing, field hockey, handball, shooting, soccer, synchronized swimming, table tennis, tennis, volleyball, water polo, weightlifting, wrestling and yachting.

Pelota – the fastest game in the world – a demonstration sport at Barcelona along with roller-hockey and taekwondo.

The Olympics is still the only competition where hundreds of millions of spectators can see some unusual sports as well as more familiar ones – all played to the highest standards.

A bird's eye view of Spain's breathtaking Montjuïc Olympic Stadium, in Barcelona, where the Games of the twenty-fifth Olympiad will take place during the summer of 1992. Montjuïc first opened in 1929. Sixty years later the rebuilt stadium reopened to stage the World Athletics Cup.

Olympic events to watch out for:	
DIVING, where, in 1988, USA's Greg Louganis hit his head on the diving board and still went on to retain two gold medals.	SOCCER, one of the world's most popular sports. At Barcelona, professional players under twenty-three will be allowed to take part.
FENCING, not the Hollywood variety, but the high-tech sword-play of real athletes not trying to kill one another, but competing for points.	TENNIS, back as an Olympic sport at Seoul in 1988, after an absence of sixty-four years – with champions Miroslav Mecir and Steffi Graf.
FIELD HOCKEY, dominated for so long by India and Pakistan, and now ruled by Olympic champions Britain.	WEIGHTLIFTING, where USSR's Alexandre Kourlovitch established himself in 1988 as the strongest man.

The Olympic events

Archery
Athletics
  All-round: decathlon, heptathlon
  Field:
    jumping (high jump, long jump, triple jump, pole vault)
    throwing (discus, hammer, javelin, shot put)
  Track:
    distance running, hurdles, middle-distance running, marathon, relays, sprinting, steeplechase
Badminton
Baseball
Basketball
Boxing
Canoeing
Cycling
Diving
Equestrian events
Fencing
Field hockey
Gymnastics
Handball
Judo
Modern pentathlon
Rowing
Shooting
Soccer
Swimming (backstroke, breaststroke, butterfly, freestyle, relays)
Synchronized swimming
Table tennis
Tennis
Volleyball
Water polo
Weightlifting
Wrestling
Yachting

Glossary

Amateur A person who takes part in a sport or activity for the love of it and not for money or as a career.
Apparatus A collection of equipment, such as the parallel bars and rings used in gymnastics.
Back straight The straight part of a running track opposite the finish line.
Boycott To refuse to have dealings with someone or an organization as a protest.
Cinder track A running track made of fine chips of rock, called cinders.
Disqualify To put out of a competition for breaking the rules.
Épée A very thin sword. When used in fencing its point is covered with a special blunt tip.
Equestrian Of or relating to horses and riding.
Medley A mixture of various types. In swimming, it refers to a race in which a different stroke is used for each length.
Olympiad A staging of the Olympic Games.
Professional A person who engages in an activity for money or as a career.
Promoter Someone who organizes and finances an event, such as a professional boxing match.
Relay A team race in which members of each team run or swim a part of the distance.
Repêchage A heat in a competition, such as fencing or rowing, in which eliminated contestants have another chance to qualify for the next round.
Reunification The act of bringing together a country that was previously divided. In 1990, East and West Germany were reunified.
Stadia Sports arenas with tiered seats.
Synthetic track A running track made of special artificial materials.
Tournament A meeting where athletes can compete against one another to determine an overall winner.
Vault To spring over an object.

Further reading

The Complete Book of the Olympics by David Wallechinsky (Penguin, 1988)
Encyclopaedia of Track and Field by Mel Watman (Hale, 1981)
The History of the Olympics (Marshall Cavendish, 1980)
Official Games Report 1988 (British Olympic Association, 1988)
The Olympians by Sebastian Coe (Pavilion, 1984)
The Olympic Games by Lord Killanin and John Rodda (Barrie and Jenkins, 1976)
The Olympic Games, Complete Track and Field Events 1896–1988 by Barry J Hugman and Peter Arnold (Arena Press, 1988)
Olympic Games, The Records by Stan Greenberg (Guinness Books, 1987)

See also titles in Wayland's *Olympic Sports* series:
Ball Sports, Combat Sports, Field Athletics, Gymnastics, Ice Sports, Skiing, Swimming and Diving and *Track Athletics.*

Index

Abrahams, Harold 40
Ali, Muhammad 8
Aouita, Said 33
Athens 5, 24, 30, 36, 40
Avdeenko, Guennadi 21
Australia 11, 13, 23, 43
    Melbourne Games 8, 39, 43

Backley, Steve 25
badminton 44
baseball 44
Beamon, Bob 28
Bikela, Abebe 31
Biondi, Matt 43
Bondarenko, Olga 14, 15
Bordin, Gelindo 31
Boutaib, Brahim 15
boxing 8-9
Britain 22, 25, 28, 40, 45
    London Games 8, 13, 24, 28, 30, 31
Bubka, Sergey 37
Bulgaria 21, 23

Canada 6, 40
    Montreal Games 6, 13, 35, 38
Caslavska, Vera 19
Chouchounova, Elena 19, 32
Christyakova, Galina 29
Cierpinski, Waldemar 31
Cuba 8, 9
cycling 10-11
Czechoslovakia 15

Davies, Lynn 28
decathlon 12-13
de Coubertin, Baron Pierre 4, 5, 44
Dillard, Harrison 22
discus 12
distance running 14-15
Dittart, Bernd 11
diving 45
Donkova, Yordanka 23

Elliott, Herb 32
equestrian events 16-17, 34, 46
Ethiopia 31

Felke, Petra 25

fencing 34, 35, 45
field hockey 45
Finland 14, 15, 24, 25
    Helsinki Games 8, 18, 21
Flintoff-King, Debbie 23
Foreman, George 8
Fortenberry, Joe 6
Fosbury, Dick 20
France 11
    Paris Games 14, 16, 18, 38
Fraser, Dawn 43
Frazier, Joe 8
Fuchs, Ruth 25

Germany
    Berlin Games 6, 43
    East 11, 25, 31, 32, 43
    Munich Games 6, 8, 19, 32, 36, 43
    reunification of 11, 17, 25, 39
    West 17, 39
Graf, Steffi 45
Griffith-Joyner, Florence 41
gymnastics 18

Hajos, Alfred 42
heptathlon 12-13
high jump 12, 13, 20-21
Hohn, Uwe 25
Holm, Eleanor 42
Holyfield, Evander 8
Hoyt, Bill 36
Hungary 8, 35, 42
hurdles 12, 13, 22-23

Italy 31
Ivan, Paula 32
Ivanov, Vyacheslav 39

Jackson, Colin 22
Japan 26, 27
    Toyko Games 26, 28, 43
javelin 12, 13, 24-25
Jenner, Bruce 12, 13
Johnson, Ben 40
Joyner-Kersee, Jackie 13, 29
Juantorena, Alberto 32
judo 26-27

Kahanamoku, Duke 42
Kano, Dr Jigoro 25
Kazankina, Tatyana 33
Kenya 15, 33
Kingdom, Roger 22
Korbut, Olga 18, 19
Korjus, Tapio 25
Kostadinova, Stefka 21
Kourlovitch, Alexandre 45
Kratochvilova, Jarmila 32
Kristiansen, Ingrid 31
Kuts, Valdimir 15

Ledovskaya, Tatyana 23
Leonard, Sugar Ray 8
Lewis, Carl 29, 40
Lewis, Lennox 8
long jump 12, 13, 28-29
Louganis, Greg 45
Louis, Spiridon 30
Lovelock, Jack 32

marathon 30-31
Martenek, Janos 35
Mathias, Bob 13
Maynard, Andrew 8
Mecir, Miroslav 45
Mercer, Ray 8
Mexico Games 20, 28
middle-distance running 12, 13, 32-33
modern pentathlon 34
Morocco 15, 33
Morris, Glenn 13
Mota, Rosa 31

New Zealand 17
Ngugi, John 15
Nordwig, Wolfgang 36
Norway 31
Nunn, Glynnis 13
Nurmi, Paavo 14, 15, 32

Onishenko, Boris 35
Otto. Kristin 43
Ovett, Steve 32
Owens, Jesse 40, 41

Papp, Laszlo 8
pelota 44
Pietri, Dorando 31
pole vault 12, 36-37
Portugal 31

Richards, Reverend Bob 36
Ritter, Louise 21
roller-hockey 44
Romania 32, 39
Rono, Peter 33
rowing 38-39

Samolenko, Tatiana 15
shot put 12, 13
Snell, Peter 32
soccer 45
South Korea 5
    Seoul Games 5, 11, 15, 17, 21, 23, 26, 29, 33, 40, 41, 43, 45
Spain 4
    Barcelona Games 4, 5, 24, 26, 44, 45
Spitz, Mark 43
sprinting 12, 13, 40-41
Stevenson, Teofilo 8, 9
Sweden
    Stockholm Games 12, 14, 16, 24, 34, 35
swimming 42-43

taekwondo 44
tennis 45
Thompson, Daley 12, 13
Todd, Mark 17
Tourischeva, Lyudmila 19

USA 6, 13, 20, 21, 22, 23, 28, 29, 36, 40, 41, 42, 43, 44
    Los Angeles Games 11, 15, 17, 21, 22, 23, 27, 29, 31
USSR 6, 11, 15, 18, 20, 29, 33
    Moscow Games 23, 27

Viren, Lasse 15

weightlifting 45
Weissmuller, Johnny 42
Whitbread, Fatima 25
Wodars, Sigrun 32
Woods, Dean 11

Yamashita, Yasuhiro 27

Zatopek, Emil 15